Prayers and Meditations
of The Mother

SRI AUROBINDO ASHRAM
PONDICHERRY

French original first published in 1932

First edition 1941
Sixth edition 1987
Second impression 1995
Third impression 1999

ISBN 81-7058-024-2

© Sri Aurobindo Ashram Trust 1987
Published by Sri Aurobindo Ashram Publication Department
Printed at All India Press, Pondicherry 605 001
PRINTED IN INDIA

Publisher's Note

The sixty-four Prayers and Meditations included in this book constitute about a fifth of the complete collection. Six of these prayers were translated by Sri Aurobindo in their entirety, three others in part. For the rest, he revised the existing translations of disciples to a greater or lesser extent. Further revisions were made when he corrected the page proofs of the first edition of the prayers in English.

The French original of *Prayers and Meditations* was published in 1932. The first edition of English translations was brought out in 1941; it contained sixty-one prayers, with an introductory note by the Mother (reproduced here in facsimile). Three more prayers were added by her to the second edition, issued in 1962. A second impression of that edition appeared in 1969, two new editions in 1971 and another in 1975. The present edition is the sixth.

Some give their soul to the Divine, some their life, some offer their work, some their money. A few consecrate all of themselves and all they have — soul, life, work, wealth; these are the true children of God. Others give nothing — these whatever their position, power and riches are for the divine purpose valueless cyphers.

This booklet is meant for those who aspire for an utter consecration to the Divine

September 1941.

November 2, 1912

Although my whole being is in theory consecrated to Thee, O Sublime Master, who art the life, the light and the love in all things, I still find it hard to carry out this consecration in detail. It has taken me several weeks to learn that the reason for this written meditation, its justification, lies in the very fact of addressing it daily to Thee. In this way I shall put into material shape each day a little of the conversation I have so often with Thee; I shall make my confession to Thee as well as it may be; not because I think I can tell Thee anything – for Thou art Thyself everything, but our artificial and exterior way of seeing and understanding is, if it may be so said, foreign to Thee, opposed to Thy nature. Still by turning towards Thee, by immersing myself in Thy light at the moment when I consider these things, little by little I shall see them more like what they really are, – until the day when, having made myself one in identity with Thee, I shall no more have anything to say to Thee, for then I shall be Thou. This is the goal that I would reach; towards this victory all my efforts will tend more and more. I aspire for the day when I can no longer say "I", for I shall be *Thou*.

How many times a day, still, I act without my action being consecrated to Thee; I at once become aware of it by an indefinable uneasiness which is translated in the sensibility of my body by a pang in my heart. I then make my action objective to myself and it seems to me ridiculous, childish or blameworthy; I deplore it, for a moment I am sad, until I dive into Thee and, there losing myself with a child's confidence, await from Thee the inspiration and strength needed to set right the error in me and around me, – two things that are one; for I have now a constant and precise perception of the universal unity determining an absolute interdependence of all actions.

November 3, 1912

Let Thy Light be in me like a Fire that makes all alive; let Thy divine Love penetrate me. I aspire with all my being for Thy reign as sovereign and master of my mind and heart and body; let them be Thy docile instruments and Thy faithful servitors.

November 19, 1912

I said yesterday to that young Englishman who is seeking for Thee with so sincere a desire, that I had definitively found Thee, that the Union was constant. Such is indeed the state of which I am conscious. All my thoughts go towards Thee, all my acts are consecrated to Thee; Thy Presence is for me an absolute, immutable, invariable fact, and Thy Peace dwells constantly in my heart. Yet I know that this state of union is poor and precarious compared with that which it will become possible for me to realise tomorrow, and I am as yet far, no doubt very far, from that identification in which I shall totally lose the notion of the "I", of that "I", which I still use in order to express myself, but which is each time a constraint, like a term unfit to express the thought that is seeking for expression. It seems to me indispensable for human communication, but all depends on what this "I" manifests; and how many times already, when I pronounce it, it is Thou who speakest in me, for I have lost the sense of separativity.

But all this is still in embryo and will continue to grow towards perfection. What an appeasing assurance there is in this serene confidence in Thy All-Might!

Thou art all, everywhere, and in all, and this body which acts is Thy own body, just as is the visible universe in its entirety; it is Thou who breathest, thinkest and lovest in this substance which, being Thyself, desires to be Thy willing servant.

November 26, 1912

What a hymn of thanksgiving should I not be raising at each moment unto Thee! Everywhere and in everything around me Thou revealest Thyself and in me Thy Will and Consciousness express themselves always more and more clearly even to the point of my having almost entirely lost the gross illusion of "me" and "mine". If a few shadows, a few flaws can be seen in the great Light which manifests Thee, how shall they bear for long the marvellous brightness of Thy resplendent Love? This morning, the consciousness that I had of the way Thou art fashioning this being which was "I" can be roughly represented by a great diamond cut with regular geometrical facets, a diamond in its cohesion, firmness, pure limpidity, transparency, but a brilliant and radiant flame in its intense ever-progressive life. But it was something more, something better than all that, for nearly all sensation inner and outer was exceeded and that image only presented itself to my mind as I returned to conscious contact with the outer world.

It is Thou that makest the experience fertile, Thou who renderest life progressive, Thou who compellest the darkness to vanish in an instant before the Light, Thou who givest to Love all its power, Thou who everywhere raisest up matter in this ardent and wonderful aspiration, in this sublime thirst for Eternity.

Thou everywhere and always; nothing but *Thou* in the essence and in the manifestation.

O Shadow and Illusion, dissolve! O Suffering, fade and disappear! Lord Supreme, art Thou not there!

November 28, 1912

The outer life, the activity of each day and each instant, is it not the indispensable complement of our hours of meditation and contemplation? And is not the proportion of time given to each the exact image of the proportion which exists between the amount of effort to be made for the preparation and realisation? For meditation, contemplation, Union is the result obtained – the flower that blooms; the daily activity is the anvil on which all the elements must pass and repass in order to be purified, refined, made supple and ripe for the illumination which contemplation gives to them. All these elements must be thus passed one after the other through the crucible before outer activity becomes needless for the integral development. Then is this activity turned into the means to manifest Thee so as to awaken the other centres of consciousness to the same dual work of the forge and the illumination. Therefore are pride and satisfaction with oneself the worst of all obstacles. Very modestly we must take advantage of all the minute opportunities offered to knead and purify some of the innumerable elements, to make them supple, to make them impersonal, to teach them forgetfulness of self and abnegation and devotion and kindness and gentleness; and when all these modes of being have become habitual to them, then are they ready to participate in the Contemplation, and to identify themselves with Thee in the supreme

Concentration. That is why it seems to me that the work must be long and slow even for the best and that striking conversions cannot be integral. They change the orientation of the being, they put it definitively on the straight path; but truly to attain the goal none can escape the need of innumerable experiences of every kind and every instant.

...O Supreme Master who shinest in my being and each thing, let Thy Light be manifest and the reign of Thy Peace come for all.

December 2, 1912

So long as one element of the being, one movement of the thought is still subjected to outside influences, not solely under Thine, it cannot be said that the true Union is realised; there is still the horrible mixture without order and light, – for that element, that movement is a world, a world of disorder and darkness, as is the entire earth in the material world, as is the material world in the entire universe.

December 3, 1912

Last night I had the experience of the effectivity of confident surrender to Thy guidance; when it is needful that something should be known, one knows it, and the more passive the mind to Thy illumination, the clearer and the more adequate is its expression.

I listened to Thee as Thou spokest in me, and I would have liked to write down what Thou saidst so that the formula in all its precision might not be lost – for now I should not be able to repeat what was said. Then I thought that this care for conservation was again an insulting lack of confidence towards Thee, for Thou canst make of me all that I need to be, and in the measure in which my attitude allows Thee to act on me and in me, Thy omnipotence has no limits. To know that at each instant what must be surely is, as perfectly as is possible, for all those who know how to see Thee in everything and everywhere! No more fear, no more uneasiness, no more anguish; nothing but a perfect Serenity, an absolute Confidence, a supreme unwavering Peace.

December 5, 1912

In Peace and Silence the Eternal manifests; allow nothing to disturb you and the Eternal will manifest; have perfect equality in face of all and the Eternal will be there.... Yes, we should not put too much intensity, too much effort into our seeking for Thee; the effort and intensity become a veil in front of Thee; we must not desire to see Thee, for that is still a mental agitation which obscures Thy Eternal Presence; it is in the most complete Peace, Serenity and Equality that all is Thou even as Thou art all, and the least vibration in this perfectly pure and calm atmosphere is an obstacle to Thy manifestation. No haste, no inquietude, no tension, Thou, nothing but Thou, without any analysis or any objectivising, and Thou art there without a possible doubt, for all becomes a Holy Peace and a Sacred Silence.

And that is better than all the meditations in the world.

December 7, 1912

Like a flame that burns in silence, like a perfume that rises straight upward without wavering, my love goes to Thee; and like the child who does not reason and has no care, I trust myself to Thee that Thy Will may be done, that Thy Light may manifest, Thy Peace radiate, Thy Love cover the world. When Thou willest I shall be in Thee, Thyself, and there shall be no more any distinction; I await that blessed hour without impatience of any kind, letting myself flow irresistibly toward it as a peaceful stream flows toward the boundless ocean.

Thy Peace is in me, and in that Peace I see Thee alone present in everything, with the calm of Eternity.

December 10, 1912

O Supreme Master, Eternal Teacher, it has been once more granted me to verify the unequalled effectivity of a full confidence in Thy leading. Thy Light was manifested through my mouth yesterday and it met no resistance in me; the instrument was willing, supple, keen of edge.

It is Thou who art the doer in each thing and each being, and he who is near enough to Thee to see Thee in all actions without exception, will know how to transform each act into a benediction.

To abide always in Thee is the one thing that matters, always and ever more and more in Thee, beyond illusions and the deceptions of the senses, not drawing back from action, refusing it, rejecting it – a struggle useless and pernicious – but living Thee alone in the act whatever it may be, ever and always Thee; then the illusion is dispelled, the falsehoods of the senses vanish, the bond of consequences is broken, all is transformed into a manifestation of the glory of Thy Eternal Presence.

So let it be. Amen.

December 11, 1912

I await, without haste, without inquietude, the tearing of another veil, the Union made more complete. I know that the veil is formed of a whole mass of small imperfections, of attachments without number.... How shall all these disappear? Slowly, as the result of countless small efforts and a vigilance not faltering even for a moment, or suddenly, through a great illumination of Thy All-Puissant Love? I know not, I do not even put to myself the question; I wait, keeping watch as best I can, in the certitude that nothing exists save Thy Will, that Thou alone art the doer and I am the instrument; and when the instrument is ready for a completer manifestation, the manifestation will quite naturally take place.

Already there is heard from behind the veil the wordless symphony of gladness that reveals Thy sublime Presence.

February 5, 1913

Thy voice is heard as a melodious chant in the stillness of my heart, and is translated in my head by words which are inadequate and yet replete with Thee. And these words are addressed to the Earth and say to her: – Poor sorrowful Earth, remember that I am present in you and lose not hope; each effort, each grief, each joy and each pang, each call of thy heart, each aspiration of thy soul, each renewal of thy seasons, all, all without exception, what seems to thee sorrowful and what seems to thee joyous, what seems to thee ugly and what seems to thee beautiful, all infallibly lead thee towards me, who am endless Peace, shadowless Light, perfect Harmony, Certitude, Rest and Supreme Blessedness.

Hearken, O Earth, to the sublime voice that arises,
Hearken and take new courage!

February 8, 1913

O Lord, Thou art my refuge and my blessing, my strength, my health, my hope, and my courage. Thou art supreme Peace, unalloyed Joy, perfect Serenity. My whole being prostrates before Thee in a gratitude beyond measure and a ceaseless worship; and that worship goes up from my heart and my mind towards Thee like the pure smoke of incense of the perfumes of India.

Let me be Thy herald among men, so that all who are ready may taste the beatitude that Thou grantest me in Thy infinite Mercy, and let Thy Peace reign upon earth.

February 10, 1913

My being goes up to Thee in thanksgiving, not because Thou usest this weak and imperfect body to manifest Thyself, but because *Thou dost manifest Thyself*, and that is the Splendour of splendours, the Joy of joys, the Marvel of marvels. All who seek Thee with ardour should understand that Thou art there whenever there is need of Thee; and if they could have the supreme faith to give up seeking Thee, but rather to await Thee, at each moment putting themselves integrally at Thy service, Thou wouldst be there whenever there was need of Thee; and is there not always need of Thee with us, whatever may be the different, and often unexpected, forms of Thy manifestation?

Let Thy glory be proclaimed,
And sanctify life;
Let it transform men's hearts,
And Thy Peace reign on earth.

February 12, 1913

As soon as all effort disappears from a manifestation, it becomes very simple, with the simplicity of a flower opening, manifesting its beauty and spreading its fragrance without clamour or vehement gesture. And in this simplicity lies the greatest power, the power which is least mixed and least gives rise to harmful reactions. The power of the vital should be mistrusted, it is a tempter on the path of the work, and there is always a risk of falling into its trap, for it gives you the taste of immediate results; and, in our first eagerness to do the work well, we let ourselves be carried away to make use of this power. But very soon it deflects all our action from the right course and introduces a seed of illusion and death into what we do.

Simplicity, simplicity! How sweet is the purity of Thy Presence!...

March 13, 1913

...Let the pure perfume of sanctification burn always, rising higher and higher, and straighter and straighter, like the ceaseless prayer of the integral being, desiring to unite with Thee so as to manifest Thee.

May 11, 1913

As soon as I have no longer any material responsibilities, all thoughts about these things flee far away from me, and I am solely and entirely occupied with Thee and Thy service. Then, in that perfect peace and serenity, I unite my will to Thine, and in that integral silence I listen to Thy truth and hear its expression. It is by becoming conscious of Thy Will and identifying ours with Thine that there is found the secret of true liberty and all-puissance, the secret of the regeneration of forces and the transfiguration of the being.

To be constantly and integrally at one with Thee is to have the assurance that we shall overcome every obstacle and triumph over all difficulties, both within and without.

O Lord, Lord, a boundless joy fills my heart, songs of gladness surge through my head in marvellous waves, and in the full confidence of Thy certain triumph I find a sovereign Peace and an invincible Power. Thou fillest my being, Thou animatest it, Thou settest in motion its hidden springs, Thou illuminest its understanding, Thou intensifiest its life, Thou increasest tenfold its love; and I no longer know whether the universe is I or I the universe, whether Thou art in me or I in Thee; Thou alone art and all is Thou; and the streams of Thy infinite grace fill and overflow the world.

Sing O lands, sing O peoples, sing O men,
The Divine Harmony is there.

June 18, 1913

To turn towards Thee, unite with Thee, live in Thee and for Thee, is supreme happiness, unmixed joy, immutable peace; it is to breathe infinity, to soar in eternity, no longer feel one's limits, escape from time and space. Why do men flee from these boons as though they fear them? What a strange thing is ignorance, that source of all suffering! How miserable that obscurity which keeps men away from the very thing which would bring them happiness and subjects them to this painful school of ordinary existence fashioned entirely from struggle and suffering!

July 21, 1913

...Yet what patience is needed! How imperceptible the stages of progress!...

Oh! how I call Thee from the very depths of my heart, True Light, Sublime Love, Divine Master who art the source of our light and of our living, our guide and our protector, the Soul of our soul and the Life of our life, the Reason of our being, the supreme Knowledge, the immutable Peace!

November 28, 1913

Mother Divine, grant that today may bring to us a completer consecration to Thy Will, a more integral gift of ourselves to Thy work, a more total forgetfulness of self, a greater illumination, a purer love. Grant that in a communion growing ever deeper, more constant and entire, we may be united always more and more closely to Thee and become Thy servitors worthy of Thee. Remove from us all egoism, root out all petty vanity, greed and obscurity. May we be all ablaze with Thy divine Love; make us Thy torches in the world.

January 24, 1914

O Thou who art the sole reality of our being, O sublime Master of love, Redeemer of life, let me have no longer any other consciousness than of Thee at every instant and in each being. When I do not live solely with Thy life, I agonise, I sink slowly towards extinction; for Thou art my only reason for existence, my one goal, my single support. I am like a timid bird not yet sure of its wings and hesitating to take its flight; let me soar to reach definitive identity with Thee.

February 1, 1914

I turn towards Thee who art everywhere and within all and outside all, intimate essence of all and remote from all, centre of condensation for all energies, creator of conscious individualities: I turn towards Thee and salute Thee, O liberator of the worlds, and, identified with Thy divine love, I contemplate the earth and its creatures, this mass of substance put into forms perpetually destroyed and renewed, this swarming mass of aggregates which are dissolved as soon as constituted, of beings who imagine that they are conscient and permanent individualities and who are as ephemeral as a breath, always alike or almost the same, in their diversity, repeating indefinitely the same desires, the same tendencies, the same appetites, the same ignorant errors.

But from time to time Thy sublime light shines in a being and radiates through him over the world, and then a little wisdom, a little knowledge, a little disinterested faith, heroism and compassion penetrates men's hearts, transforms their minds and sets free a few elements from that sorrowful and implacable wheel of existence to which their blind ignorance subjects them.

But how much greater a splendour than all that have gone before, how marvellous a glory and light would be needed to draw these beings out of the horrible aberration in which they are plunged by the life of cities and so-called civilisations! What a formidable and, at the same time, divinely sweet puissance would be needed to turn aside all these wills from the bitter struggle for their selfish, mean and foolish satisfactions, to snatch them from this vortex which hides death behind its treacherous glitter, and turn them towards Thy conquering harmony!

O Lord, eternal Master, enlighten us, guide our steps, show us the way towards the realisation of Thy law, towards the accomplishment of Thy work.

I adore Thee in silence and listen to Thee in a religious concentration.

February 14, 1914

Peace, peace upon all the earth!

May all escape from the ordinary consciousness and be delivered from the attachment for material things; may they awake to the knowledge of Thy divine presence, unite themselves with Thy supreme consciousness and taste the plenitude of peace that springs from it.

Lord, Thou art the sovereign Master of our being. Thy law is our law, and with all our strength we aspire to identify our consciousness with Thy eternal consciousness, that we may accomplish Thy sublime work in each thing and at every moment.

Lord, deliver us from all care for contingencies, deliver us from the ordinary outlook on things. Grant that we may henceforth see only with Thy eyes and act only by Thy will. Transform us into living torches of Thy divine love.

With reverence, with devotion, in a joyful consecration of my whole being I give myself, O Lord, to the fulfilment of Thy law.

Peace, peace upon all the earth!

February 15, 1914

O Thou, sole Reality, Light of our light and Life of our life, Love supreme, Saviour of the world, grant that more and more I may be perfectly awakened to the awareness of Thy constant presence. Let all my acts conform to Thy law; let there be no difference between my will and Thine. Extricate me from the illusory consciousness of my mind, from its world of fantasies; let me identify my consciousness with the Absolute Consciousness, for that art Thou.

Give me constancy in the will to attain the end, give me firmness and energy and the courage which shakes off all torpor and lassitude.

Give me the peace of perfect disinterestedness, the peace that makes Thy presence felt and Thy intervention effective, the peace that is ever victorious over all bad will and every obscurity.

Grant, I implore Thee, that all in my being may be identified with Thee. May I be nothing else any more than a flame of love utterly awakened to a supreme realisation of Thee.

March 7, 1914

> *On Board the Kaga Maru*

This morning my prayer rises to Thee, always with the same aspiration: to live Thy love, to radiate Thy love, with such potency and effectiveness that all may feel fortified, regenerated and illumined by our contact. To have power to heal life, to relieve suffering, to generate peace and calm confidence, to efface anguish and replace it by the sense of the one true happiness, the happiness that is founded in Thee and never fades....

O Lord, O marvellous Friend, O all-powerful Master, penetrate all our being, transfigure it till Thou alone livest in us and through us.

March 8, 1914

In front of this calm sunrise which turned all within me into silence and peace, at the moment when I grew conscious of Thee and Thou alone wast living in me, O Lord, it seemed to me that I adopted all the inhabitants of this ship, and enveloped them in an equal love, and that so in each one of them something of Thy consciousness would awake. Not often had I felt so strongly Thy divine power, and Thy invincible light, and once again total was my confidence and unmixed my joyful surrender.

O Thou who relievest all suffering and dispersest all ignorance, O Thou the supreme healer, be constantly present on this boat in the heart of those whom it shelters that once again Thy glory may be manifested!

March 9, 1914

Those who live for Thee and in Thee may change their physical surroundings, their habits, climate, "milieu", but everywhere they find the same atmosphere; they carry that atmosphere in themselves, in their thought constantly fixed on Thee. Everywhere they feel at home, for everywhere they are in Thy house. No longer do they marvel at the novelty, unexpectedness, picturesqueness of things and countries; for them, it is Thy presence that is manifest in all and Thy unchangeable splendour which never leaves them, is apparent in the least grain of sand. The whole earth chants Thy praises; in spite of the obscurity, misery, ignorance, through it all, it is still the glory of Thy love which we perceive and with which we can commune ceaselessly everywhere.

O Lord, my sweet Master, all this I constantly experience on this boat which seems to me a marvellous abode of peace, a temple sailing in Thy honour over the waves of the subconscient passivity which we have to conquer and awaken to the consciousness of Thy divine Presence.

Blessed was the day when I came to know Thee, O Ineffable Eternity.

Blessed among all days be that day when the earth at last awakened shall know Thee and shall live only for Thee.

March 25, 1914

Silent and unseen as always, but all-powerful, Thy action has made itself felt and, in these souls that seemed to be so closed, a perception of Thy divine light is awake. I knew well that none could invoke Thy presence in vain and if in the sincerity of our hearts we commune with Thee through no matter what organism, body or human collectivity, this organism in spite of its ignorance finds its unconsciousness wholly transformed. But when in one or several elements there is the conscious transformation, when the flame that smoulders under the ashes leaps out suddenly illumining all the being, then with joy we salute Thy sovereign action, testify once more to Thy invincible puissance and can hope that a new possibility of true happiness has been added to the others in mankind.

O Lord, an ardent thanksgiving mounts from me towards Thee expressing the gratitude of this sorrowing humanity which Thou illuminest, transformest and glorifiest and givest to it the peace of Knowledge.

April 10, 1914

Suddenly the veil was rent, the horizon was disclosed – and before the clear vision my whole being threw itself at Thy feet in a great outburst of gratitude. Yet in spite of this deep and integral joy all was calm, all was peaceful with the peace of eternity.

I seem to have no more limits; there is no longer the perception of the body, no sensations, no feelings, no thoughts – a clear, pure, tranquil immensity penetrated with love and light, filled with an unspeakable beatitude is all that is there and that alone seems now to be myself, and this "myself" is so little the former "I", selfish and limited, that I cannot tell if it is I or Thou, O Lord, sublime Master of our destinies.

It is as though all were energy, courage, force, will, infinite sweetness, incomparable compassion....

Even more forcibly than during these last days the past is dead and as though buried under the rays of a new life. The last glance that I have just thrown backward as I read a few pages of this book definitely convinced me of this death, and lightened of a great weight I present myself before Thee, O my divine Master, with all the simplicity, all the nudity of a child.... And still the one only thing I perceive is that calm and pure immensity....

Lord, Thou hast answered my prayer, Thou hast granted me what I have asked from Thee; the "I" has disappeared, there is only a docile instrument put at Thy service, a centre of concentration and manifestation of Thy infinite and eternal rays; Thou hast taken my life and made it Thine; Thou hast taken my will and hast united it to Thine; Thou hast taken my love and identified it with Thine; Thou hast taken my thought and replaced it by Thy absolute consciousness.

The body, marvelling, bows its forehead in the dust in mute and submissive adoration.

And nothing else exists but Thou alone in the splendour of Thy immutable peace.

April 17, 1914

O Lord, O almighty Master, sole Reality, grant that no error, no obscurity, no fatal ignorance may creep into my heart and my thought.

In action, the personality is the inevitable and indispensable intermediary of Thy will and Thy forces.

The stronger, the more complex, powerful, individualised and conscious is the personality, the more powerfully and usefully can the instrument serve. But, by reason of the very character of personality, it easily tends to be drawn into the fatal illusion of its separate existence and become little by little a screen between Thee and that on which Thou willest to act. Not at the beginning, in the manifestation, but in the transmission of the return; that is to say, instead of being, as a faithful servant, an intermediary who brings back to Thee exactly what is Thy due – the forces sent forth in reply to Thy action, – there is a tendency in the personality to want to keep for itself a part of the forces, with this idea: "It is I who have done this or that, I who am thanked...." Pernicious illusion, obscure falsehood, now are you discovered and unmasked. That is the maleficent canker corroding the fruit of the action, falsifying all its results.

O Lord, O my sweet Master, sole Reality, dispel this feeling of the "I". I have now understood that so long as there will be a manifested universe, the "I" will remain necessary for Thy manifestation; to dissolve, or even to diminish or weaken the "I", is to deprive Thee of the means of manifestation, in whole or part. But what must be radically and definitively suppressed is the illusory thought, the illusory feeling, the illusory sensation of the separate "I". At no moment, in no circumstances must we forget that our "I" has no reality outside Thee.

O my sweet Master, my divine Lord, tear out from my heart this illusion so that Thy servant may become pure and faithful and faithfully and integrally bring back to Thee all that is Thy due. In silence let me contemplate and understand this supreme ignorance and dispel it for ever. Chase the shadow from my heart, and let Thy light reign in it, its uncontested sovereign.

May 12, 1914

More and more it seems to me that we are in one of those periods of activity in which the fruit of past efforts becomes apparent, – a period in which we act according to Thy law in the measure in which it is the sovereign controller of our being, without having even the leisure to become conscious of the law.

This morning passing by a rapid experience from depth to depth, I was able, once again, as always, to identify my consciousness with Thine and to live no longer in aught but Thee; – indeed, it was Thou alone that was living, but immediately Thy will pulled my consciousness towards the exterior, towards the work to be done, and Thou saidst to me, "Be the instrument of which I have need." And is not this the last renunciation, to renounce identification with Thee, to renounce the sweet and pure joy of no longer distinguishing between Thee and me, the joy of knowing at each moment, not only with the intellect but by an integral experience, that Thou art the unique Reality and that all the rest is but appearance and illusion. That the exterior being should be the docile instrument which does not even need to be conscious of the will which moves it, is not doubtful; but why must I be almost entirely identified with the instrument and why should not the "I" be entirely merged in Thee and live Thy full and absolute consciousness?

I ask, but I am not anxious about it. I know that all is according to Thy will, and with a pure adoration I trust myself joyously to Thy will. I shall be what Thou wouldst have me be, O Lord, conscient or inconscient, a simple instrument as is the body or a supreme knowledge as art Thou. O the sweet and peaceful joy when one can say "All is good" and feel Thee at work in the world through all the elements which lend themselves to that transmission.

Thou art the sovereign Master of all, Thou art the Inaccessible, the Unknowable, the eternal and sublime Reality.

O marvellous Unity, I disappear in Thee.

May 21, 1914

Outside all manifestation, in the immutable silence of Eternity, I am in Thee, O Lord, an unmoving beatitude. In that which, out of Thy puissance and marvellous light, forms the centre and reality of the atoms of matter I find Thee; thus without going out of Thy Presence I can disappear in Thy supreme consciousness or see Thee in the radiant particles of my being. And for the moment that is the plenitude of Thy life and Thy illumination.

I see Thee, I am Thyself, and between these two poles my intense love aspires towards Thee.

May 22, 1914

When we have discerned successively what is real from what is unreal in all the states of being and all the worlds of life, when we have arrived at the perfect and integral certitude of the sole Reality, we must turn our gaze from the heights of this supreme consciousness towards the individual aggregate which serves as the immediate instrument for Thy manifestation upon earth, and see in it nothing but Thee, our sole real existence. Thus each atom of this aggregate will be awakened to receive Thy sublime influence; the ignorance and the darkness will disappear not only from the central consciousness of the being but also from its most external mode of expression. It is only by the fulfilment, by the perfection of this labour of transfiguration that there can be manifested the plenitude of Thy Presence, Thy Light and Thy Love.

Lord, Thou makest me understand this truth ever more clearly; lead me step by step on that path. My whole being down to its smallest atom aspires for the perfect knowledge of Thy presence and a complete union with it. Let every obstacle disappear, let Thy divine knowledge replace in every part the darkness of the ignorance. Even as Thou hast illumined the central consciousness, the will in the being, enlighten too this outermost substance. And let the whole individuality, from its first origin and essence to its last projection and most material body, be unified in a perfect realisation and a complete manifestation of Thy sole Reality.

Nothing is in the universe but Thy Life, Thy Light, Thy Love.

Let everything become resplendent and transfigured by the knowledge of Thy Truth.

Thy divine love floods my being; Thy supreme light is shining in every cell; all exults because it knows Thee and because it is one with Thee.

May 26, 1914

On the surface is the storm, the sea is in turmoil, waves clash and leap one on another and break with a mighty uproar. But all the time, under this water in fury, are vast smiling expanses, peaceful and motionless. They look upon the surface agitation as an indispensable act; for matter has to be vigorously churned if it is to become capable of manifesting entirely the divine light. Behind the troubled appearance, behind the struggle and anguish of the conflict, the consciousness remains firm at its post; observing all the movements of the outer being, it intervenes only to rectify direction and position, so as not to allow the play to become too dramatic. This intervention is now firm and a little severe, now ironical, a call to order or a mockery, full always of a strong, gentle, peaceful and smiling benevolence.

In the silence I beheld Thy infinite and eternal Beatitude.

Then softly a prayer rises towards Thee from what is still in the shadow and the struggle: O sweet Master, O supreme Giver of illumination and purity, grant that all substance and every activity may be no more anything other than a constant manifestation of Thy divine Love and Thy sovereign Serenity....

And in my heart is the song of gladness of Thy sublime magnificence.

August 27, 1914

To be the divine love, love powerful, infinite, unfathomable, in every activity, in all the worlds of being – it is for this I cry to Thee, O Lord. Let me be consumed with this love divine, love powerful, infinite, unfathomable, in every activity, in all the worlds of being! Transmute me into that burning brazier so that all the atmosphere of earth may be purified with its flame.

O, to be Thy Love infinitely....

August 31, 1914

In this formidable disorder and terrible destruction can be seen a great working, a necessary toil preparing the earth for a new sowing which will rise in marvellous spikes of grain and give to the world the shining harvest of a new race.... The vision is clear and precise, the plan of Thy divine law so plainly traced that peace has come back and installed itself in the hearts of the workers. There are no more doubts and hesitations, no longer any anguish or impatience. There is only the grand straight line of the work eternally accomplishing itself in spite of all, against all, despite all contrary appearances and illusory detours. These physical personalities, moments unseizable in the infinite Becoming, know that they will have made humanity take one farther step, infallibly and without care for the inevitable results, whatever be the apparent momentary consequences: they unite themselves with Thee, O Master eternal, they unite themselves with Thee, O Mother universal, and in this double identity with That which is beyond and That which is all the manifestation they taste the infinite joy of the perfect certitude.

Peace, peace in all the world....
War is an appearance,
Turmoil is an illusion,
Peace is there, immutable peace.

Mother, sweet Mother who I am, Thou art at once the destroyer and the builder.

The whole universe lives in Thy breast with all its life innumerable and Thou livest in Thy immensity in the least of its atoms.

And the aspiration of Thy infinitude turns towards That which is not manifested to cry to it for a manifestation ever more complete and more perfect.

All *is*, in one time, in a triple and clairvoyant total Consciousness, the Individual, the Universal, the Infinite.

September 1, 1914

O Mother Divine, with what fervour, what ardent love I came to Thee in Thy deepest consciousness, in Thy high status of sublime love and perfect felicity, and I nestled so close into Thy arms and loved Thee with so intense a love that I became altogether Thyself. Then in the silence of our mute ecstasy a voice from yet profounder depths arose and the voice said, "Turn towards those who have need of thy love." All the grades of consciousness appeared, all the successive worlds. Some were splendid and luminous, well ordered and clear; there knowledge was resplendent, expression was harmonious and vast, will was potent and invincible. Then the worlds darkened in a multiplicity more and more chaotic, the Energy became violent and the material world obscure and sorrowful. And when in our infinite love we perceived in its entirety the hideous suffering of the world of misery and ignorance, when we saw our children locked in a sombre struggle, flung upon each other by energies that had deviated from their true aim, we willed ardently that the light of Divine Love should be made manifest, a transfiguring force at the centre of these distracted elements. Then, that the will might be yet more powerful and effective, we turned towards Thee, O unthinkable Supreme, and we implored Thy aid. And from the unsounded depths of the Unknown a reply came sublime and formidable and we knew that the earth *was saved*.

September 25, 1914

O Divine and adorable Mother, with Thy help what is there that is impossible? The hour of realisations is near and Thou hast assured us of Thy aid that we may perform integrally the supreme Will.

Thou hast accepted us as fit intermediaries between the unthinkable realities and the relativities of the physical world, and Thy constant presence in our midst is a token of Thy active collaboration.

> The Lord has willed and Thou dost execute:
> A new Light shall break upon the earth.
> A new world shall be born,
> And the things that were announced shall be fulfilled.

September 28, 1914

My pen is mute to chant Thy presence, O Lord; yet art Thou like a king who has taken entire possession of his kingdom. Thou art there, organising, putting all in place, developing and increasing every province. Thou awakenest those that were asleep. Thou makest active those that were sinking towards inertia; Thou art building a harmony out of the whole. A day will come when the harmony shall be achieved and all the country shall be by its very life the bearer of Thy word and Thy manifestation.

But meanwhile my pen is mute to chant Thy praise.

September 30, 1914

O Thou, Sublime Love, to whom I gave never any other name but who art so wholly the very substance of my being, Thou whom I feel vibrant and alive in the least of my atoms even as in the infinite universe and beyond, Thou who breathest in every breath, movest in the heart of all activities, art radiant through all that is of good will and hidden behind all sufferings, Thou for whom I cherish a cult without limit which grows ever more intense, permit that I may with more and more reason feel that I am Thyself wholly.

And Thou, O Lord, who art all this made one and much more, O sovereign Master, extreme limit of our thought, who standest for us at the threshold of the Unknown, make rise from that Unthinkable some new splendour, some possibility of a loftier and more integral realisation, that Thy work may be accomplished and the universe take one step farther towards the sublime Identity, the supreme Manifestation.

And now my pen falls mute and I adore Thee in silence.

October 5, 1914

In the calm silence of Thy contemplation, O Divine Master, Nature is fortified and tempered anew. All principle of individuality is overpassed, she is plunged in Thy infinity that allows oneness to be realised in all domains without confusion, without disorder. The combined harmony of that which persists, that which progresses and that which eternally is, is little by little accomplished in an always more complex, more extended and more lofty equilibrium. And this interchange of the three modes of life allows the plenitude of the manifestation.

Many seek Thee at this hour in anguish and incertitude. May I be their mediator with Thee that Thy light may illumine them, that Thy peace may appease. My being is now only a point of support for Thy action and a centre for Thy consciousness. Where now are the limits, whither have fled the obstacles? Thou art the sovereign Lord of Thy kingdom.

October 7, 1914

Oh, let Light be poured on all the earth and Peace inhabit every heart.... Almost all know only the material life heavy, inert, conservative, obscure; their vital forces are so tied to this physical form of existence that, even when left to themselves and outside the body, they are still solely occupied with these material contingencies that are yet so harassing and painful.... Those in whom the mental life is awakened are restless, tormented, agitated, arbitrary, despotic. Caught altogether in the whirl of the renewals and transformations of which they dream, they are ready to destroy everything without knowledge of any foundation on which to construct and with their light made only of blinding flashes they increase yet more the confusion rather than help it to cease.

In all there lacks the unchanging peace of Thy sovereign contemplation and the calm vision of Thy immutable eternity.

And with the infinite gratitude of the individual being to whom Thou hast accorded this surpassing grace, I implore Thee, O Lord, that under cover of the present turmoil, in the very heart of this extreme confusion the miracle may be accomplished and Thy law of supreme serenity and pure unchanging light become visible to the perception of all and govern the earth in a humanity at last awakened to Thy divine consciousness.

O sweet Master, Thou hast heard my prayer, Thou wilt reply to my call.

October 14, 1914

Mother Divine, Thou art with us; every day Thou givest me the assurance and, closely united in an identity that grows more and more total, more and more constant, we turn to the Lord of the Universe and to That which is beyond in a great aspiration towards the new Light. All the earth is in our arms like a sick child who must be cured and for whom one has a special affection because of his very weakness. Cradled on the immensity of the eternal becomings, ourselves those becomings, we contemplate hushed and glad the eternity of the immobile Silence where all is realised in the perfect Consciousness and immutable Existence, miraculous gate of all the unknown that is beyond.

Then is the veil torn, the inexpressible Glory uncovered and, suffused with the ineffable Splendour, we turn back towards the world to bring it the glad tidings.

Lord, Thou hast given me the happiness infinite. What being, what circumstances can have the power to take it away from me?

October 25, 1914

My aspiration to Thee, O Lord, has taken the form of a beautiful rose, harmonious, full in bloom, rich in fragrance. I stretch it out to Thee with both arms in a gesture of offering and I ask of Thee: If my understanding is limited, widen it; if my knowledge is obscure, enlighten it; if my heart is empty of ardour, set it aflame; if my love is insignificant, make it intense; if my feelings are ignorant and egoistic, give them the full consciousness in the Truth. And the "I" which demands this of Thee, O Lord, is not a little personality lost amidst thousands of others. It is the whole earth that aspires to Thee in a movement full of fervour.

In the perfect silence of my contemplation all widens to infinity, and in the perfect peace of that silence Thou appearest in the resplendent glory of Thy Light.

November 8, 1914

For the plenitude of Thy Light we invoke Thee, O Lord! Awaken in us the power to express Thee.

All is mute in the being as in a desert crypt; but in the heart of the shadow, in the bosom of the silence burns the lamp that can never be extinguished, the fire of an ardent aspiration to know Thee and totally to live Thee.

The nights follow the days, new dawns unweariedly succeed to past dawns, but always there mounts the scented flame that no storm-wind can force to vacillate. Higher it climbs and higher and one day attains the vault still closed, the last obstacle opposing our union. And so pure, so erect, so proud is the flame that suddenly the obstacle is dissolved.

Then Thou appearest in all Thy splendour, in the dazzling force of Thy infinite glory; at Thy contact the flame changes into a column of light that chases the shadows away for ever.

And the Word leaps forth, a supreme revelation.

February 15, 1915

O Lord of Truth, thrice have I implored Thy manifestation invoking Thee with deep fervour.

Then, as always, the whole being made its total submission. At that moment the consciousness perceived the individual being mental, vital and physical, covered all over with dust, and this being lay prostrate before Thee, its forehead touching the earth, dust in the dust, and it cried to Thee, "O Lord, this being made of dust prostrates itself before Thee praying to be consumed with the fire of the Truth that it may henceforth manifest only Thee." Then thou saidst to it, "Arise, thou art pure of all that is dust." And suddenly, in a stroke, all the dust sank from it like a cloak that falls on the earth, and the being appeared erect, always as substantial but resplendent with a dazzling light.

March 3, 1915

Solitude, a harsh intense solitude, and always this strong impression of having been flung headlong into a hell of darkness! Never at any moment of my life, in any circumstances have I felt myself living in surroundings so entirely opposite to all that I am conscious of as true, so contrary to all that is the essence of my life. Sometimes when the impression and the contrast grow very intense, I cannot prevent my total submission from taking on a hue of melancholy and the calm and mute converse with the Master within is transformed for a moment into an invocation that almost supplicates, "O Lord, what have I done that Thou hast thrown me thus into the sombre Night?" But immediately the aspiration rises, still more ardent, "Spare this being all weakness; suffer it to be the docile and clear-eyed instrument of Thy work, whatever that work may be."

March 7, 1915

I am exiled from every spiritual happiness, and of all ordeals this, O Lord, is surely the most painful that Thou canst impose: but most of all the withdrawal of Thy will which seems to be a sign of total disapprobation. Strong is the growing sense of rejection, and it needs all the ardour of an untiring faith to keep the external consciousness thus abandoned to itself from being invaded by an irremediable sorrow....

But it refuses to despair, it refuses to believe that the misfortune is irreparable; it waits with humility in an obscure and hidden effort and struggle for the breath of Thy perfect joy to penetrate it again. And perhaps each of its modest and secret victories is a true help brought to the earth....

If it were possible to come definitively out of this external consciousness, to take refuge in the divine consciousness! But that Thou hast forbidden and still and always Thou forbidst it. No flight out of the world! The burden of its darkness and ugliness must be borne to the end even if all divine succour seems to be withdrawn. I must remain in the bosom of the Night and walk on without compass, without beacon-light, without inner guide.

I will not even implore Thy mercy; for what Thou willst for me, I too will. All my energy is in tension solely to advance, always to advance step after step, despite the depth of the darkness, despite the obstacles of the way, and whatever comes, O Lord, it is with a fervent and unchanging love that Thy decision will be welcomed. Even if Thou findest the instrument unfit to serve Thee, the instrument belongs to itself no more, it is Thine; Thou canst destroy or magnify it, it exists not in itself, it wills nothing, it can do nothing without Thee.

March 8, 1915

For the most part the condition is one of calm and profound indifference; the being feels neither desire nor repulsion, neither enthusiasm nor depression, neither joy nor sorrow. It regards life as a spectacle in which it takes only a very small part; it perceives its actions and reactions, conflicts and forces as things that at once belong to its own existence which overflows the small personality on every side and yet to that personality are altogether foreign and remote.

But from time to time a great breath passes, a great breath of sorrow, of anguished isolation, of spiritual destitution, – one might almost say, the despairing appeal of Earth abandoned by the Divine. It is a pang as silent as it is cruel, a sorrow submissive, without revolt, without any desire to avoid or pass out of it and full of an infinite sweetness in which suffering and felicity are closely wedded, something infinitely vast, great and deep, too great, too deep perhaps to be understood by men – something that holds in it the seed of To-morrow....

December 26, 1916

Always the word Thou makest me hear in the silence is sweet and encouraging, O Lord. But I see not in what this instrument is worthy of the grace Thou accordest to it or how it will have the capacity to realise what Thou attendest from it. All in it appears so small, weak and ordinary, so lacking in intensity and force and amplitude in comparison with what it should be to undertake this overwhelming role. But I know that what the mind thinks is of little importance. The mind itself knows it and, passive, it awaits the working out of Thy decree.

Thou biddest me strive without cease, and I could wish to have the indomitable ardour that prevails over every difficulty. But Thou hast put in my heart a peace so smiling that I fear I no longer know even how to strive. Things develop in me, faculties and activities, as flowers bloom, spontaneously and without effort, in a joy to be and a joy to grow, a joy to manifest Thee, whatever the mode of Thy manifestation. If struggle there is, it is so gentle and easy that it can hardly be given the name. But how small is this heart to contain so great a love! and how weak this vital and physical being to carry the power to distribute it! Thus Thou hast placed me on the threshold of the marvellous Way, but will my feet have the strength to advance upon it?... But Thou repliest to me that my movement is to soar and it would be an error to wish to walk.... O Lord, how infinite is Thy compassion! Once more Thou hast taken me in Thy omnipotent arms and cradled me on Thy unfathomable heart, and Thy heart said to me, "Torment not thyself at all, be confident like a child: art thou not myself crystallised for my work?"

December 27, 1916

O my beloved Lord, my heart is bowed before Thee, my arms are stretched towards Thee imploring Thee to set all this being on fire with Thy sublime love that it may radiate from there on the world. My heart is wide open in my breast; my heart is open and turned towards Thee, it is open and empty that Thou mayest fill it with Thy divine Love; it is empty of all but Thee and Thy presence fills it through and through and yet leaves it empty, for it can contain also all the infinite variety of the manifested world....

O Lord, my arms are outstretched in supplication towards Thee, my heart is wide open before Thee, that Thou mayest make of it a reservoir of Thy infinite love.

"Love me in all things, everywhere and in all beings" was Thy reply. I prostrate myself before Thee and ask of Thee to give me that power.

December 29, 1916

O my sweet Lord, teach me to be the instrument of Thy Love.

March 30, 1917

There is a sovereign royalty in taking no thought for oneself. To have needs is to assert a weakness; to claim something proves that we lack what we claim. To desire is to be impotent; it is to recognise our limitations and confess our incapacity to overcome them. If only from the point of view of a legitimate pride, man should be noble enough to renounce desire. How humiliating to ask something for oneself from life or from the Supreme Consciousness which animates it! How humiliating for us, how ignorant an offence against Her! For all is within our reach, only the egoistic limits of our being prevent us from enjoying the whole universe as completely and concretely as we possess our own body and its immediate surroundings.

March 31, 1917

Each time that a heart leaps at the touch of Thy divine breath, a little more beauty seems to be born upon the Earth, the air is embalmed with a sweet perfume, all becomes more friendly.

How great is Thy power, O Lord of all existences, that an atom of Thy joy is sufficient to efface so much darkness, so many sorrows and a single ray of Thy glory can light up thus the dullest pebble, illumine the blackest consciousness!

Thou hast heaped Thy favours upon me, Thou hast unveiled to me many secrets, Thou hast made me taste many unexpected and unhoped for joys, but no grace of Thine can be equal to this Thou grantest to me when a heart leaps at the touch of Thy divine breath.

At these blessed hours all earth sings a hymn of gladness, the grasses shudder with pleasure, the air is vibrant with light, the trees lift towards heaven their most ardent prayer, the chant of the birds becomes a canticle, the waves of the sea billow with love, the smile of children tells of the infinite and the souls of men appear in their eyes.

Tell me, wilt Thou grant me the marvellous power to give birth to this dawn in expectant hearts, to awaken the consciousness of men to Thy sublime presence, and in this bare and sorrowful world awaken a little of Thy true Paradise? What happiness, what riches, what terrestrial powers can equal this wonderful gift!

O Lord, never have I implored Thee in vain, for that which speaks to Thee is Thyself in me.

Drop by drop Thou allowest to fall in a fertilising rain the living and redeeming flame of Thy almighty love. When these drops of eternal light descend softly on our world of obscure ignorance, one would say a rain upon earth of golden stars one by one from a sombre firmament.

All kneels in mute devotion before this ever-renewed miracle.

April 7, 1917

A deep concentration seized on me, and I perceived that I was identifying myself with a single cherry-blossom, then through it with all cherry-blossoms, and, as I descended deeper in the consciousness, following a stream of bluish force, I became suddenly the cherry-tree itself, stretching towards the sky like so many arms its innumerable branches laden with their sacrifice of flowers. Then I heard distinctly this sentence:

"Thus hast thou made thyself one with the soul of the cherry-trees and so thou canst take note that it is the Divine who makes the offering of this flower-prayer to heaven."

When I had written it, all was effaced; but now the blood of the cherry-tree flows in my veins and with it flows an incomparable peace and force. What difference is there between the human body and the body of a tree? In truth, there is none: the consciousness which animates them is identically the same.

Then the cherry-tree whispered in my ear:

"It is in the cherry-blossom that lies the remedy for the disorders of the spring."

April 28, 1917

O my divine Master, who hast appeared to me this night in all Thy radiant splendour, Thou canst in an instant make this being perfectly pure, luminous, translucid, conscious. Thou canst liberate it from its last dark spots, free it from its last preferences. Thou canst... but hast Thou not done this tonight when it was penetrated with Thy divine effluence and Thy ineffable light? It may be... for in me is a superhuman strength made all of calm and immensity. Grant that from this summit I may not fall; grant that peace may for ever reign as the master of my being, not only in my depths of which it has long been the sovereign but in the least of my external activities, in the smallest recesses of my heart and of my action.

I salute Thee, O Lord, deliverer of beings!

"Lo! here are flowers and benedictions! here is the smile of divine Love! It is without preferences and without repulsions. It streams out towards all in a generous flow and never takes back its marvellous gifts!"

Her arms outstretched in a gesture of ecstasy, the Eternal Mother pours upon the world the unceasing dew of Her purest love!

September 24, 1917

Thou hast subjected me to a hard discipline; rung after rung, I have climbed the ladder which leads to Thee and, at the summit of the ascent, Thou hast made me taste the perfect joy of identity with Thee. Then, obedient to Thy command, rung after rung, I have descended to outer activities and external states of consciousness, re-entering into contact with these worlds that I left to discover Thee. And now that I have come back to the bottom of the ladder, all is so dull, so mediocre, so neutral, in me and around me, that I understand no more....

What is it then that Thou awaitest from me, and to what use that slow long preparation, if all is to end in a result to which the majority of human beings attain without being subjected to any discipline?

How is it possible that having seen all that I have seen, experienced all that I have experienced, after I have been led up even to the most sacred sanctuary of Thy knowledge and communion with Thee, Thou hast made of me so utterly common an instrument in such ordinary circumstances? In truth, O Lord, Thy ends are unfathomable and pass my understanding....

Why, when Thou hast placed in my heart the pure diamond

of Thy perfect Felicity, sufferest Thou its surface to reflect the shadows which come from outside and so leave unsuspected and, it would seem, ineffective the treasure of Peace Thou hast granted me? Truly all this is a mystery and confounds my understanding.

Why, when Thou hast given me this great inner silence, sufferest Thou the tongue to be so active and the thought to be occupied with things so futile? Why?... I could go on questioning indefinitely and, to all likelihood, always in vain....

I have only to bow to Thy decree and accept my condition without uttering a word.

I am now only a spectator who watches the dragon of the world unrolling its coils without end.

October 15, 1917

I have cried to Thee in my despair, O Lord, and Thou hast answered my call.

I have no right to complain of the circumstances of my existence; are they not consonant with what I am?

Because Thou ledst me to the threshold of Thy splendour and gavest me the joy of Thy harmony, I thought I had reached the goal: but, in truth, Thou hast regarded Thy instrument in the perfect clarity of Thy light and plunged it back into the crucible of the world that it may be melted anew and purified.

In these hours of an extreme and anguished aspiration I see, I feel myself drawn by Thee with a dizzy rapidity along the road of transformation and my whole being vibrates to a conscious contact with the Infinite.

It is so that Thou givest me patience and the strength to surmount this new ordeal.

November 25, 1917

O Lord, because in an hour of cruel distress I said in the sincerity of my faith: "Thy Will be done," Thou camest garbed in Thy raiment of glory. At Thy feet I prostrated myself, on Thy breast I found my refuge. Thou hast filled my being with Thy divine light and flooded it with Thy bliss. Thou hast reaffirmed Thy alliance and assured me of Thy constant presence. Thou art the sure friend who never fails, the Power, the Support, the Guide. Thou art the Light which scatters darkness, the Conqueror who assures the victory. Since Thou art there, all has become clear. Agni is rekindled in my fortified heart, and his splendour shines out and sets aglow the atmosphere and purifies it....

My love for Thee, compressed so long, has leaped forth again, powerful, sovereign, irresistible – increased tenfold by the ordeal it has undergone. It has found strength in its seclusion, the strength to emerge to the surface of the being, impose itself as master on the entire consciousness, absorb everything in its overflowing stream....

Thou hast said to me: "I have returned to leave thee no more."

And, my forehead on the soil, I have received Thy promise.

July 12, 1918

Suddenly, before Thee, all my pride fell. I understood how futile it was in Thy Presence to wish to surmount oneself, and I wept, wept abundantly and without constraint the sweetest tears of my life. Tears sweet and beneficent, tears that opened my heart without constraint before Thee and melted in one miraculous moment all the remaining obstacles that could separate me from Thee!

And now, although I weep no longer, I feel so near, so near to Thee that my whole being quivers with joy.

Let me stammer out my homage:

I have cried too with the joy of a child, "O supreme and only Confidant, Thou who knowest beforehand all we can say to Thee because Thou art its source!

"O supreme and only Friend, Thou who acceptest, Thou who lovest, Thou who understandest us just as we are, because it is Thyself who hast so made us!

"O supreme and only Guide, Thou who never gainsayest our highest will because it is Thou Thyself who willest in it!

"It would be folly to seek elsewhere than in Thee for one who will listen, understand, love and guide, since always Thou art there ready to our call and never wilt Thou fail us!

"Thou hast made me know the supreme, the sublime joy of a perfect confidence, an absolute serenity, a surrender total and without reserve or colouring, free from effort and constraint.

"Joyous like a child I have smiled and wept at once before Thee, O my Well-Beloved!"

September 3, 1919

Since the man refused the meal I had prepared with so much love and care, I invoked the God to take it.

My God, Thou hast accepted my invitation, Thou hast come to sit at my table, and in exchange for my poor and humble offering Thou hast granted to me the last liberation. My heart, even this morning so heavy with anguish and care, my head surcharged with responsibility, are delivered of their burden. Now are they light and joyful as my inner being has been for a long time past. My body smiles to Thee with happiness as before my soul smiled to Thee. And surely hereafter Thou wilt withdraw no more from me this joy, O my God! for this time, I think, the lesson has been sufficient, I have mounted the calvary of successive disillusionments high enough to attain to the Resurrection. Nothing remains of the past but a potent love which gives me the pure heart of a child and the lightness and freedom of thought of a god.

June 22, 1920

After granting me the joy which surpasses all expression, Thou hast sent me, O my beloved Lord, the struggle, the ordeal and on this too I have smiled as on one of Thy precious messengers. Before, I dreaded the conflict, for it hurt in me the love of harmony and peace. But now, O my God, I welcome it with gladness: it is one among the forms of Thy action, one of the best means for bringing back to light some elements of the work which might otherwise have been forgotten, and it carries with it a sense of amplitude, of complexity, of power. And even as I have seen Thee, resplendent, exciting the conflict, so also it is Thou whom I see unravelling the entanglement of events and jarring tendencies and winning in the end the victory over all that strives to veil Thy light and Thy power: for out of the struggle it is a more perfect realisation of Thyself that must arise.

November 24, 1931

O my Lord, my sweet Master, for the accomplishment of Thy work I have sunk down into the unfathomable depths of Matter, I have touched with my finger the horror of the falsehood and the inconscience, I have reached the seat of oblivion and a supreme obscurity. But in my heart was the Remembrance, from my heart there leaped the call which could arrive to Thee: "Lord, Lord, everywhere Thy enemies appear triumphant; falsehood is the monarch of the world; life without Thee is a death, a perpetual hell; doubt has usurped the place of Hope and revolt has pushed out submission; Faith is spent, Gratitude is not born; blind passions and murderous instincts and a guilty weakness have covered and stifled Thy sweet law of love. Lord, wilt Thou permit Thy enemies to prevail, falsehood and ugliness and suffering to triumph? Lord, give the command to conquer and victory will be there. I know we are unworthy, I know the world is not yet ready. But I cry to Thee with an absolute faith in Thy Grace and I know that Thy Grace will save."

Thus, my prayer rushed up towards Thee; and, from the depths of the abyss, I beheld Thee in Thy radiant splendour; Thou didst appear and Thou saidst to me: "Lose not courage, be firm, be confident, – I COME."

October 23, 1937

(A prayer for those who wish to serve the Divine)

Glory to Thee, O Lord, who triumphest over every obstacle.

Grant that nothing in us shall be an obstacle in Thy work.

Grant that nothing may retard Thy manifestation.

Grant that Thy will may be done in all things and at every moment.

We stand here before Thee that Thy will may be fulfilled in us, in every element, in every activity of our being, from our supreme heights to the smallest cells of the body.

Grant that we may be faithful to Thee utterly and for ever.

We would be completely under Thy influence to the exclusion of every other.

Grant that we may never forget to own towards Thee a deep, an intense gratitude.

Grant that we may never squander any of the marvellous things that are Thy gifts to us at every instant.

Grant that everything in us may collaborate in Thy work and all be ready for Thy realisation.

Glory to Thee, O Lord, Supreme Master of all realisation.

Give us a faith active and ardent, absolute and unshakable in Thy Victory.